Preschool Skills

Same and Different

Illustrations by Holli Conger

An imprint of Sterling Children's Books

FLASH KIDS, STERLING, and the distinctive Sterling logo are registered trademarks of
Sterling Publishing Co., Inc.

Published by Sterling Publishing Co., Inc.
387 Park Avenue South, New York, NY 10016
Text and illustrations © 2005 by Flash Kids
Distributed in Canada by Sterling Publishing
c/o Canadian Manda Group, 165 Dufferin Street
Toronto, Ontario, Canada M6K 3H6
Distributed in the United Kingdom by GMC Distribution Services
Castle Place, 166 High Street, Lewes, East Sussex, England BN7 1XU
Distributed in Australia by Capricorn Link (Australia) Pty. Ltd.
P.O. Box 704, Windsor, NSW 2756, Australia

Sterling ISBN 978-1-4114-3426-4

Manufactured in Canada

Lot #:
6 8 10 9 7
03/12

For information about custom editions, special sales, premium and
corporate purchases, please contact Sterling Special Sales
Department at 800-805-5489 or specialsales@sterlingpublishing.com.

Cover illustrations, design, and production by Mada Design, Inc.

Dear Parent,

Help your child build a solid educational foundation with this Preschool Skills workbook. Colorful illustrations and fun activities introduce the concept of same and different. Understanding this concept is key to understanding larger concepts, such as sorting and classifying things. Your child will enjoy completing matching activities and coloring the fun illustrations. Help your child make the most of this workbook with these tips:

- Provide a quiet, comfortable place for your child to complete this workbook. Go through each page with him or her slowly to ensure full comprehension of each activity.

- If your child answers a question incorrectly, explain why it is incorrect and allow your child to correct the mistake.

- Encourage your child to ask questions and have discussions about the things your child finds interesting in this book. You can also ask your child questions to keep him or her engaged in learning.

- Try to relate things found in this book to things your child encounters in everyday life. This will strengthen the connection between words and everyday objects.

- Most of all, enjoy this special time spent together! Reading to your child and helping him or her learn will build a strong bond between you both.

Tasty Treats

Circle the object in each row
that is the **same** as the first one.

Fun on the Farm

Circle the object in each row
that is the **same** as the first one.

Cool Clothes

Circle the object that is **different** in each row.

School Supplies

Circle the object that is **different** in each row.

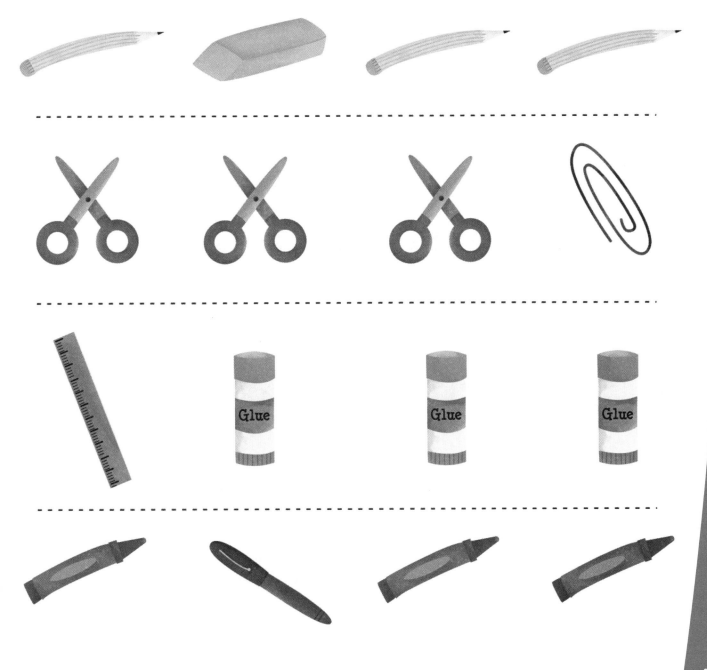

So Many Shoes

Circle the object in each row
that is the **same** as the first one.

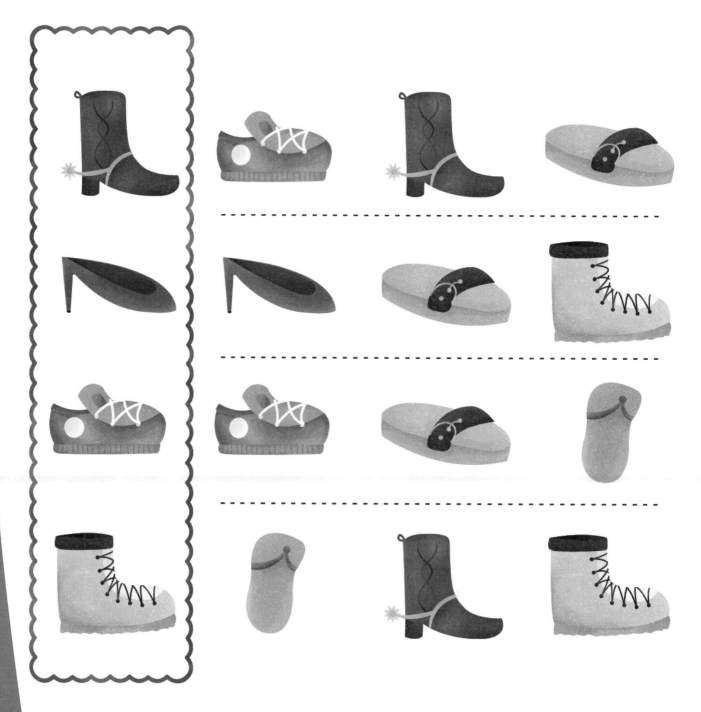

At the Beach

Circle the object in each row
that is the **same** as the first one.

Happy Hamsters

Circle the object that is **different** in each row.

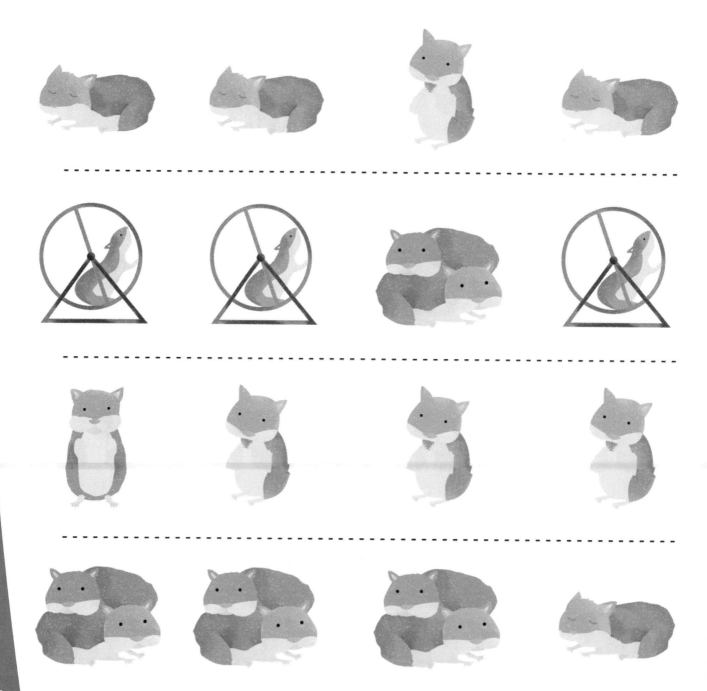

Terrific Toys

Circle the object that is **different** in each row.

Fun with Fruit

Circle the object in each row
that is the **same** as the first one.

Furry Friends

Circle the object in each row
that is the **same** as the first one.

Time for Lunch

Circle the object that is **different** in each row.

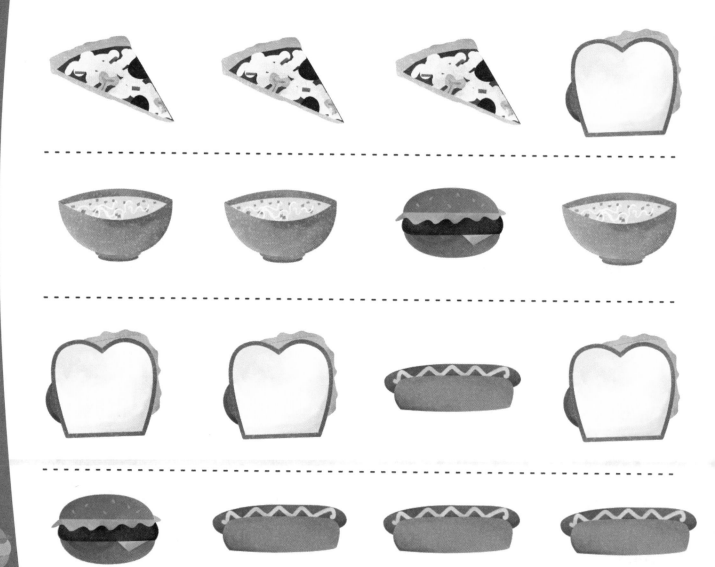

Zoo Animals

Circle the object that is **different** in each row.

What's for Breakfast?

Circle the two pictures that are the **same** in each group.

Girls and Boys

Circle the two pictures that are the **same** in each group.

The Great Outdoors

Circle the picture that is **different** in each group.

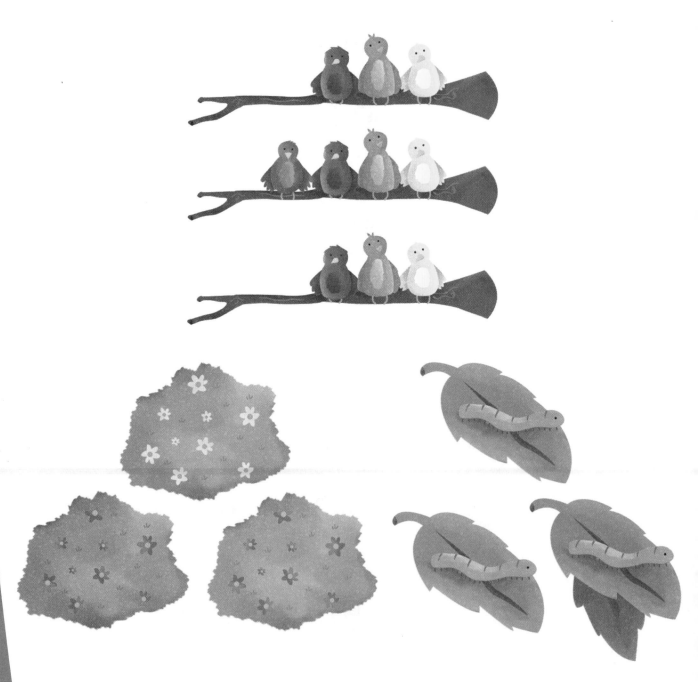

Party Time

Circle the picture that is **different** in each group.

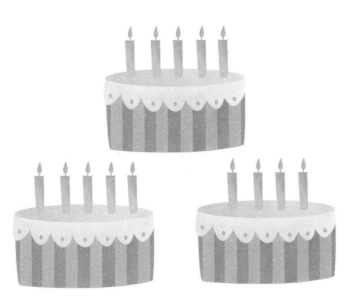

19

At the Circus

Circle the two pictures that are the **same** in each group.

Delicious Dessert

Circle the two pictures that are the **same** in each group.

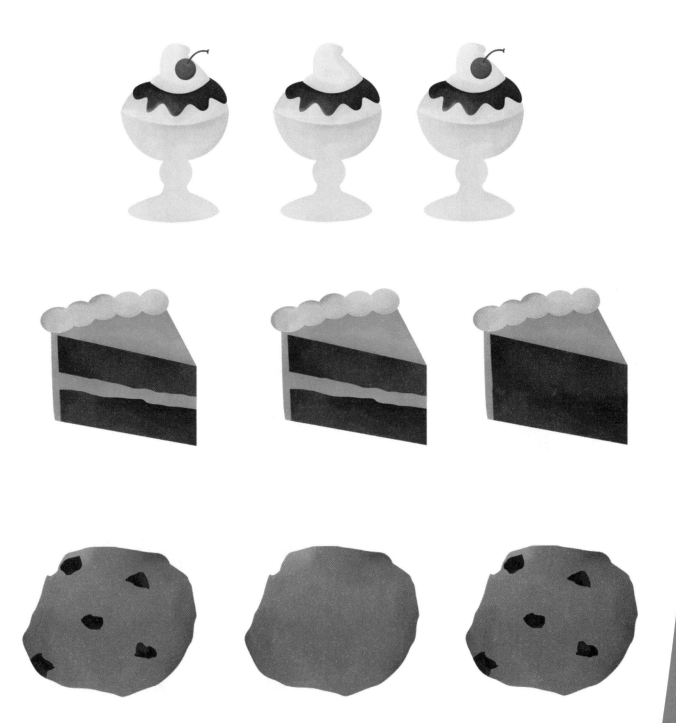

Many Monkeys

Circle the picture that is **different** in each group.

Cuddly Cats

Circle the picture that is **different** in each group.

Baby Animals

Circle the picture in each row
that **belongs** with the first one.

Play Time

Circle the picture in each row
that **belongs** with the first one.

Lots of Clothes

Circle the picture that
does not belong in each row.

Amazing Animals

Circle the picture that
does not belong in each row.

School Time

Circle the picture in each row
that **belongs** with the first one.

Yummy Treats

Circle the picture in each row
that **belongs** with the first one.

Around the House

Circle the picture that **does not belong** in each row.

Getting Around

Circle the picture that
does not belong in each row.

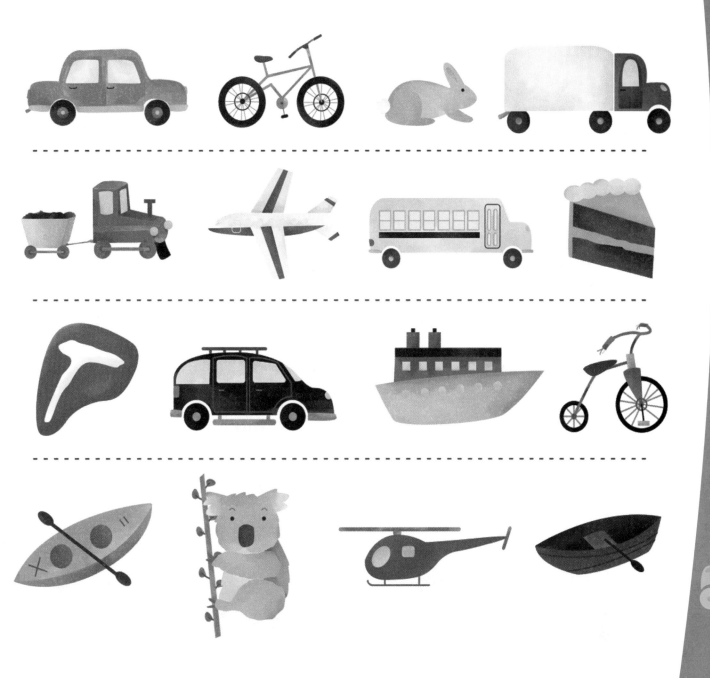

Hooray for Hats

Circle the object in each row that is the **same color** as the first one.

Super Sports

Circle the object in each row that is the **same color** as the first one.

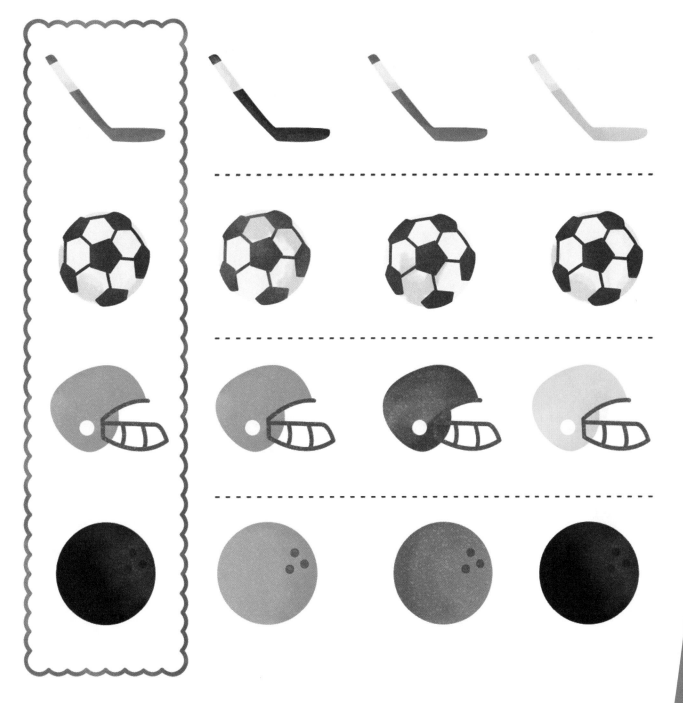

Having Fun

Circle the object that is
a **different color** in each row.

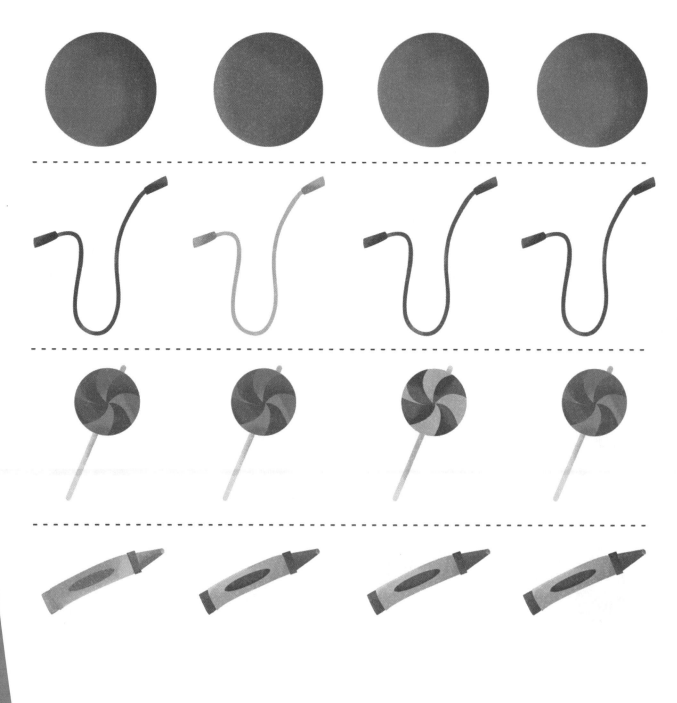

A Trip to the Farm

Circle the object that is
a **different color** in each row.

Pretty Petals

Color the first flower in each row.
Then color the flower that is
the **same** as the first one.

Color the Kids

Color the first child in each row.
Then color the child who is
the **same** as the first one.

Crazy for Candy

Color the object that is **different** in each row.

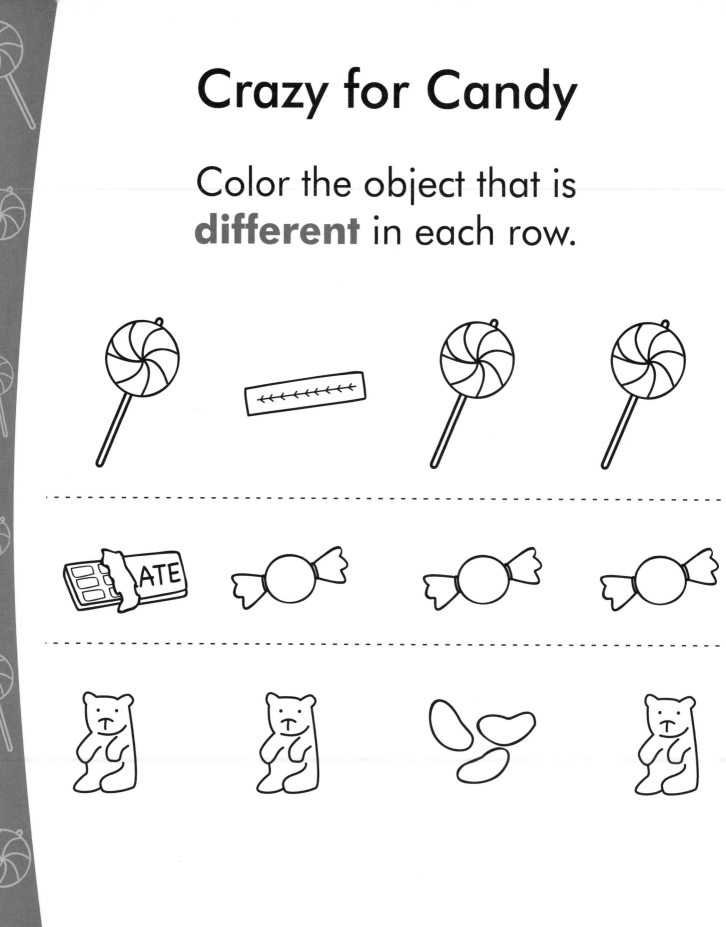

Eat Your Veggies

Color the object that is **different** in each row.

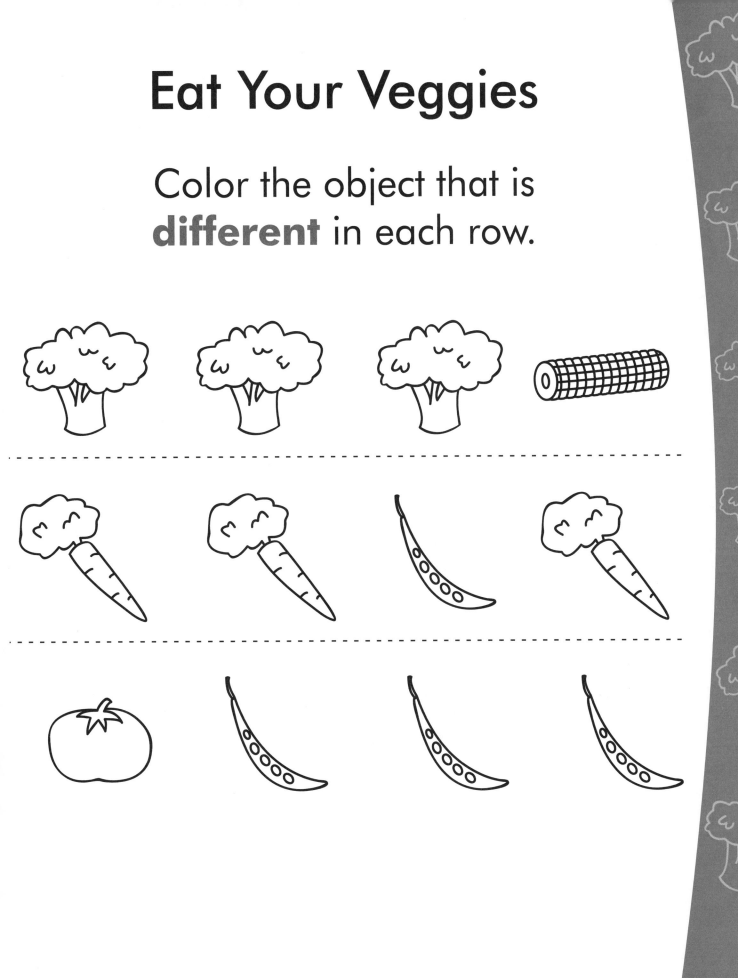

Ship Shape

Circle the shape in each row that is the **same** as the first one.

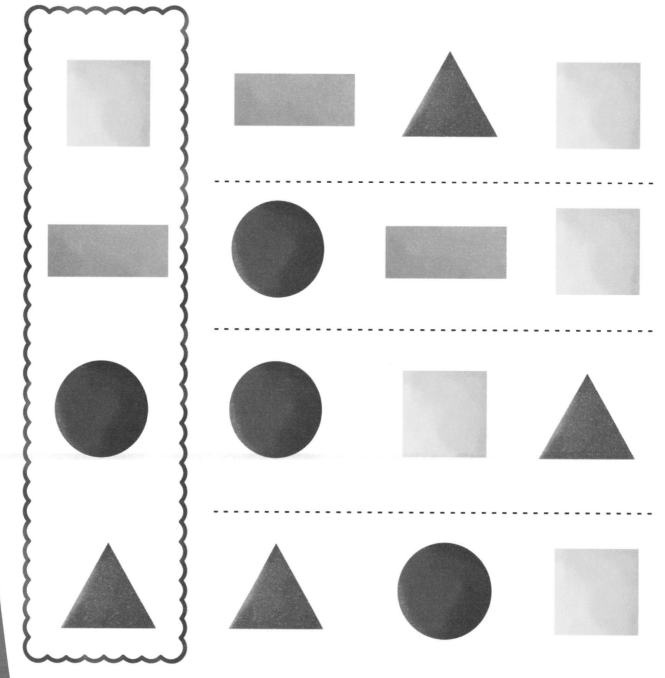

So Many Shapes

Circle the shape in each row that is the **same** as the first one.

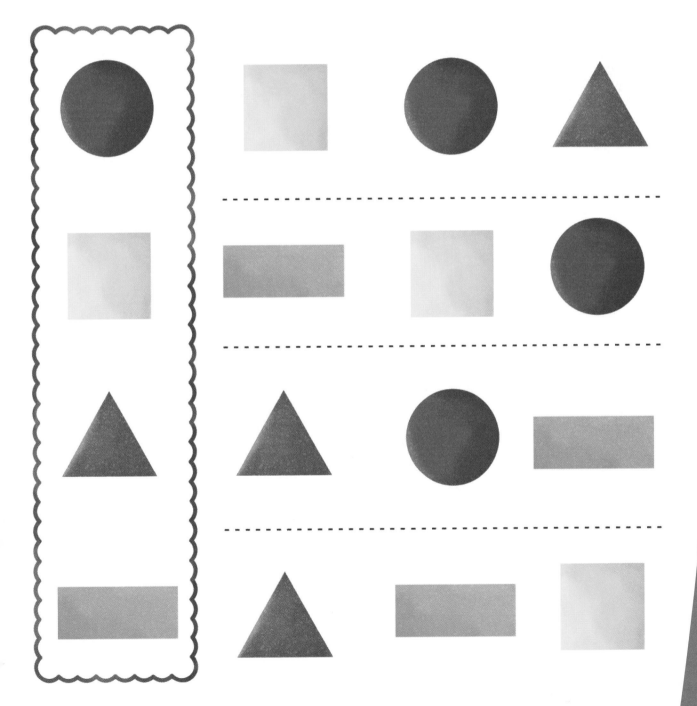

Super Shapes

Circle the shape that is **different** in each row.

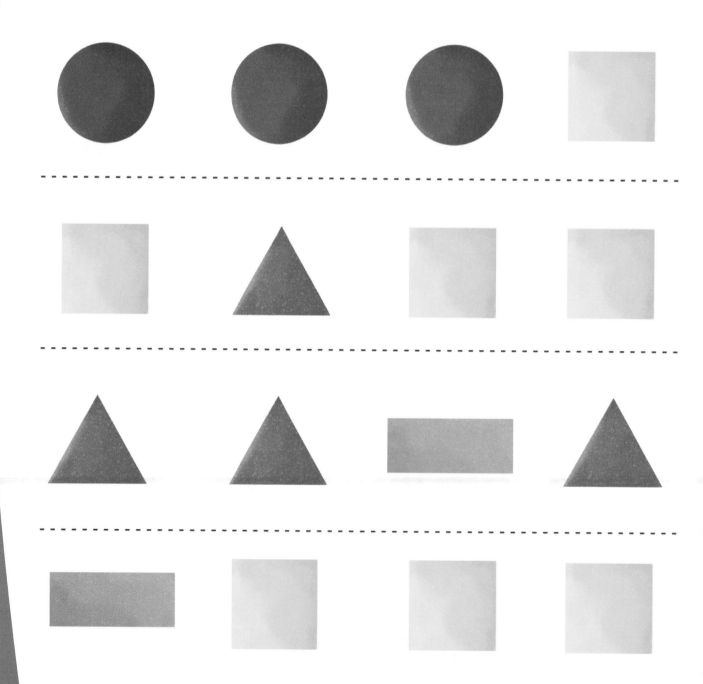

Some More Shapes

Circle the shape that is **different** in each row.

Squares

Circle the objects on the page that are the **same shape** as the first one.

Circles

Circle the objects on the page that are the **same shape** as the first one.

Triangles

Circle the objects on the page that are a **different shape** than the first one.

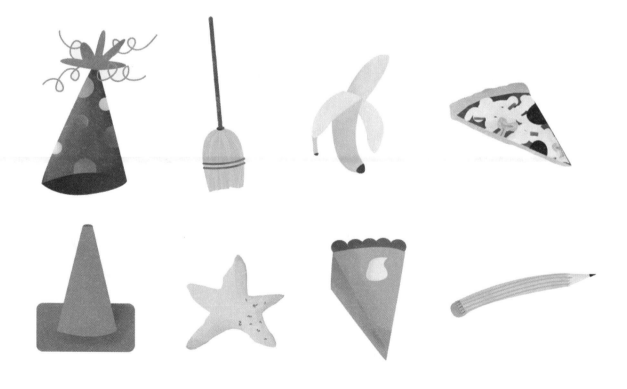

46

Rectangles

Circle the objects on the page that are a **different shape** than the first one.

How Many Lollipops?

Circle the number in each row that is the **same** as the first one.

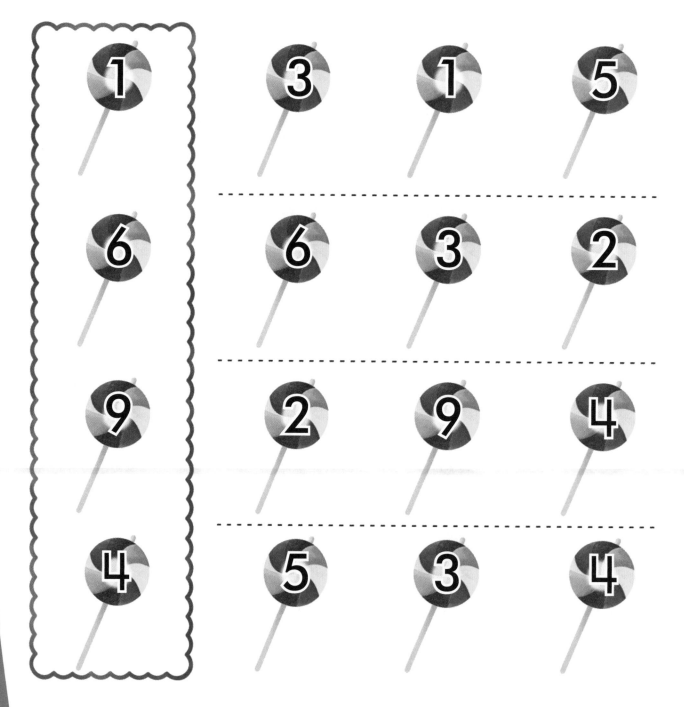

1	3	1	5
6	6	3	2
9	2	9	4
4	5	3	4

How Many Flowers?

Circle the number in each row that is the **same** as the first one.

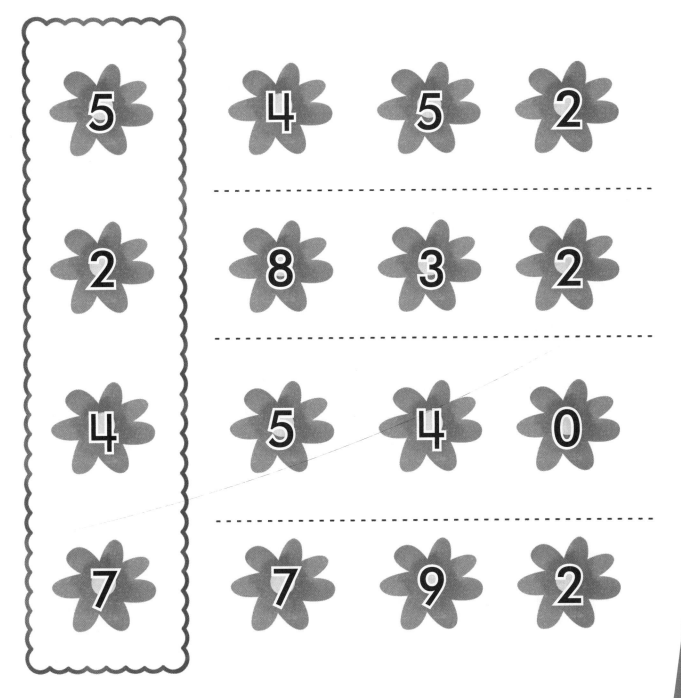

49

How Many Eggs?

Circle the number that is **different** in each row.

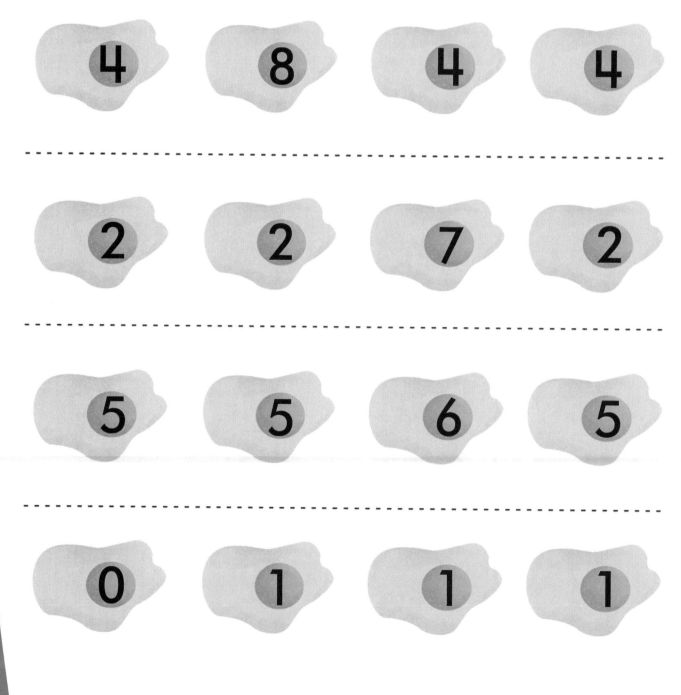

4 8 4 4

2 2 7 2

5 5 6 5

0 1 1 1

How Many Pigs?

Circle the number that is **different** in each row.

Yellow Bees

Color the objects on the page that show the **same number** as the first one.

Yummy Cookies

Color the objects on the page that show the **same number** as the first one.

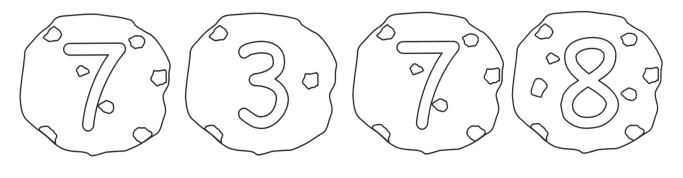

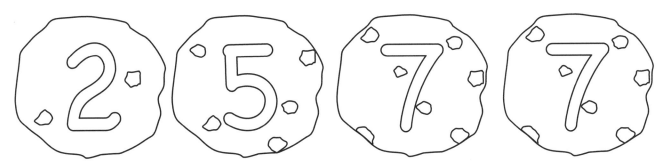

Green Leaves

Color the objects on the page that show **different number** than the first one.

Tiny Ants

Color the objects on the page that show a **different number** than the first one.

Bugs in the Garden

Circle the object in each row that is the **same size** as the first one.

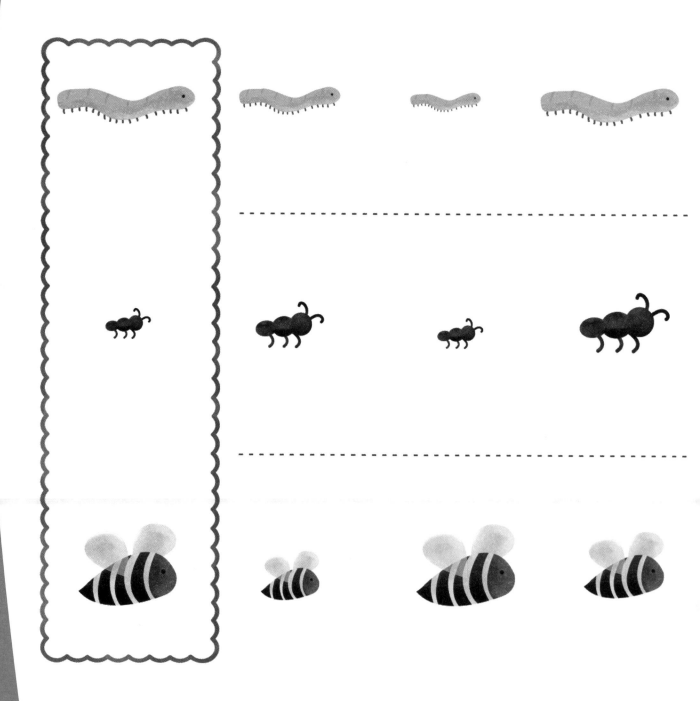

A Day in the Sun

Circle the object in each row that is the **same size** as the first one.

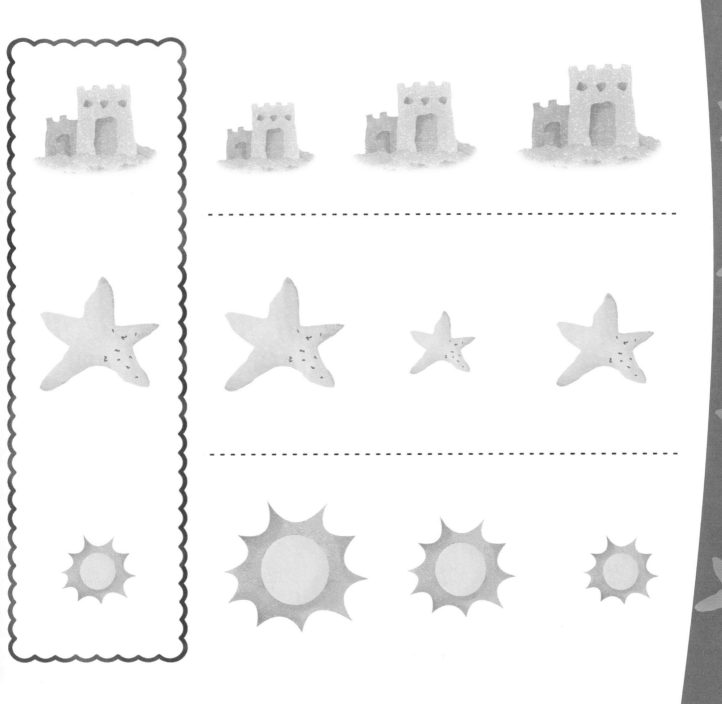

Sweet Treats

Circle the object that is
a **different size** in each row.

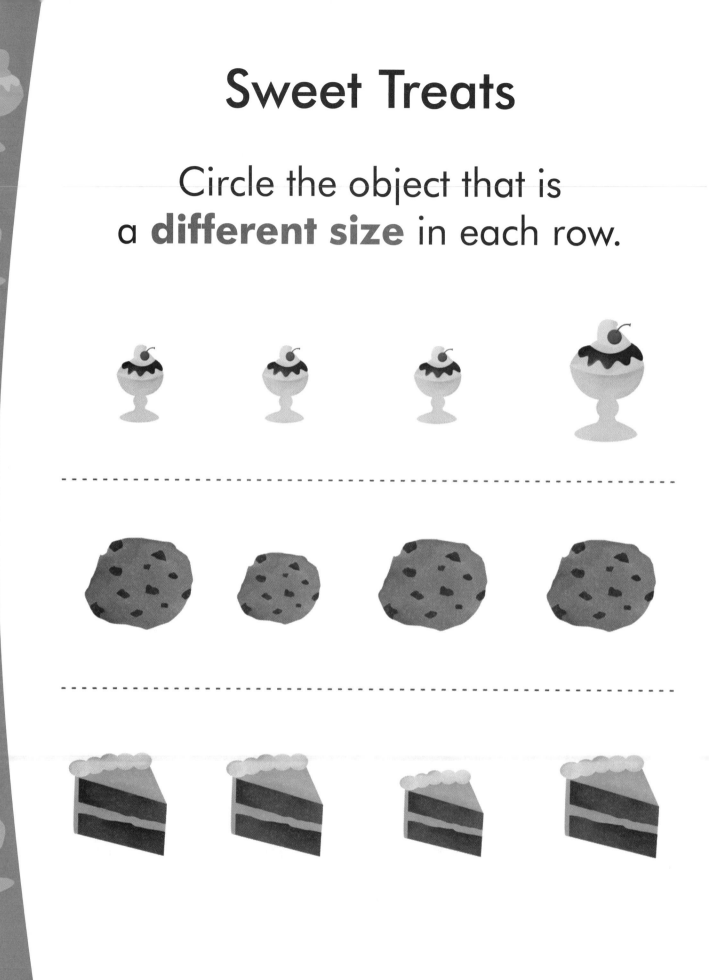

Ready for School

Circle the object that is
a **different size** in each row.

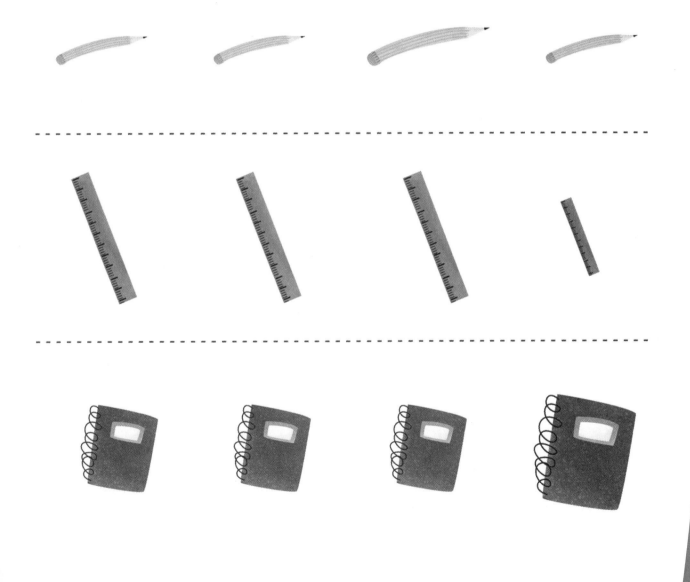

Giraffes Are Great

Color the objects on the page that are the **same size** as the first one.

A Cool Clown

Color the objects on the page that are the **same size** as the first one.

61

A Super Sneaker

Color the objects on the page that are a **different size** than the first one.

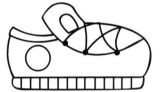 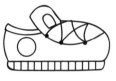 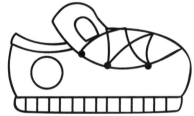 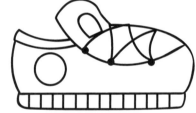

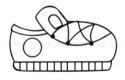 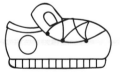 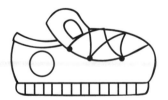 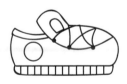

A Funny Monkey

Color the objects on the page that are a **different size** than the first one.

63

_____ '
(Name)

you did a great job
learning about
same and different!